SEGEDUNUM
ROMAN FORT, BATHS & MUSEUM

The entrance to Segedunum Roman Fort, Baths and Museum.

Segedunum is one of the most fully excavated fort sites anywhere in the Roman Empire, and certainly on Hadrian's Wall.

Following a £9 million development the site has become a major new visitor attraction on Tyneside. Altogether it took three and a half years from the commencement of the first excavation, on the site of the bath-house in January 1997, to the opening of the museum in June 2000.

Segedunum has won four awards in its first year since opening, including *Northumbria Family Attraction of the Year* 2001 (Good Britain Guide) and the British Archaeological Awards *Heritage in Britain Trophy* for 2000.

Segedunum is composed of a number of distinct elements, all combining to inform and delight any visitor wishing to know more of the history of Hadrian's Wall and the settlement that has become Wallsend.

Contents

His Royal Highness the Duke of Edinburgh meeting members of re-enactment group *Cohors Quinta Gallorum* in the bath-house at Segedunum.

Construction work at Segedunum Roman Fort, as depicted in one of the museum's models.

Segedunum, the Roman fort at Wallsend, marks the eastern end of Hadrian's Wall, for almost 300 years the north-west frontier of the once mighty Roman Empire.

It is from its Roman past that Wallsend takes its name, but the town is equally famous as a world leader in both coal mining and shipbuilding.

The impact of the Roman and industrial ages can be seen today at the site, a vivid testimony to Wallsend's changing role in the world.

This guide aims to provide the reader with an account of the history of Wallsend, and a description of the displays and remains to be seen at Segedunum, which include reconstructions of a section of Hadrian's Wall and a typical Roman military bath-house as well as a spectacularly collapsed section of Hadrian's Wall, a late eighteenth century colliery and the ground plan of the fort of Segedunum itself.

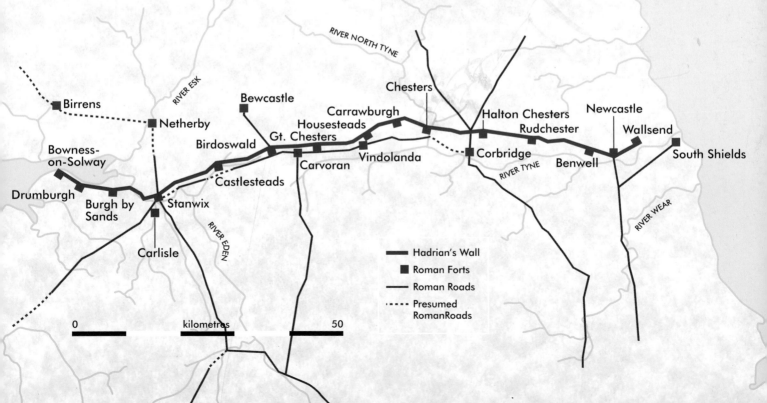

RIVER NORTH TYNE

RIVER ESK

Birrens

Netherby

Bewcastle

Chesters

Carrawburgh

Housesteads

Halton Chesters

Newcastle

Birdoswald

Gt. Chesters

Rudchester

Wallsend

Bowness-on-Solway

Carvoran

Vindolanda

Corbridge

South Shields

Drumburgh

Castlesteads

Benwell

Burgh by Sands

Stanwix

RIVER TYNE

Carlisle

RIVER EDEN

RIVER WEAR

	Hadrian's Wall
	Roman Forts
	Roman Roads
	Presumed RomanRoads

0   kilometres   50

Main image: Artist's impression of Segedunum
Roman Fort AD 200, looking up-river towards
Newcastle upon Tyne.
ENGLISH HERITAGE / PAINTED BY PETER DUNN

Left inset: Archaeologists revealing ard (an early type of plough)
marks which show the site of the fort was under cultivation
before the Roman army arrived.

History

The fort is situated on a plateau overlooking the north bank of the river Tyne, at a point where it turns eastwards to run to the coast at South Shields. The site was chosen to command views eastwards down the river as far as South Shields, and two miles upriver towards Newcastle.

Little is known about prehistoric activity at Wallsend, but it is clear that there must have been some form of settlement in the area as the site of the fort was under cultivation immediately before Roman construction work began. The fields seem to have been prepared for the growing season when they were taken over, as freshly dug furrows were filled in by the Romans to form a construction platform for the fort.

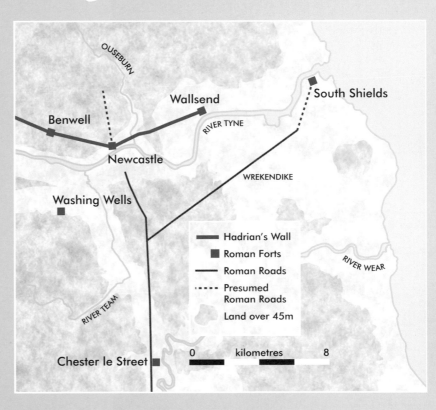

Key:

- **Hadrian's Wall**
- ■ Roman Forts
- —— Roman Roads
- ····· Presumed Roman Roads
- Land over 45m

0   kilometres   8

The building of Hadrian's Wall

Main image: View west along Hadrian's Wall from Walltown Crags area.
LM KAY

Left inset: The Roman Empire in Hadrian's reign. It covered much of the then known world.

Britannia

R. Rhine

Germania

Gallia

R. Danube

Hispania

Roma

R. Euphrates

R. Tigris

Mediterranean Sea

Syria

Aegyptus

R. Nile

Although Julius Caesar had raided southern Britain as early as 55 BC, it was not until AD 43 that the Roman invasion took place. At first efforts were concentrated in the south, but by the AD 80s the Roman army had reached the Tyne. However, no occupation is known at Wallsend before the construction of Hadrian's Wall in the AD 120s.

All that is known from Roman histories about the construction of the Wall is that Hadrian 'erected a wall along a length of 80 miles which was to separate barbarians and Romans'. Everything we know about the Wall today is the result of work by archaeologists.

Emperor Hadrian

Originally the Wall was to have been 10 Roman feet wide (a Roman foot is 295mm and is slightly smaller than an Imperial foot), with a fortlet every mile and a turret every third of a mile. At some point during the building, a whole series of forts were added to the line, often resulting in the demolition of half finished towers and sections of the Wall. In addition, the width of the Wall was reduced to eight Roman feet.

At its east end the Wall was originally planned to end at Newcastle, in Roman times, as today, the lowest bridging point of the river Tyne.

HADRIAN

Born in AD 76, Hadrian became Emperor in AD 117 and ruled the Roman Empire for the next 21 years. He is generally regarded as having been an extremely effective Emperor, with administrative reforms, as well as extensive building programmes, taking place throughout the Empire under his reign. However, it is perhaps his frontier policies that have attracted most attention.

Unlike previous Emperors, Hadrian was a voracious traveller, and conducted a full tour of the provinces of his Empire, causing him to be away from Rome for years at a time. He introduced a policy of consolidation of the frontiers, even abandoning some of the eastern conquests of his predecessor Trajan. In some respects his policy was simply the formalisation of increasingly static frontier lines that had evolved over the previous 50 years, but remains of the systems established by him can still be seen today on the Rhine and Danube rivers, in Africa, and in Britain in particular.

Hadrian's Wall provides the most powerful testimony to the Emperor's policy. Elsewhere rivers and deserts formed the frontiers, and although linear barriers were erected in places, none could compare with the sheer scale of Hadrian's Wall. Today, almost 1,900 years since its creation, the Wall is now a World Heritage Site. It gained this status, accorded to only a handful of monuments in Britain, because of its remarkable preservation, and because it is still such a powerful symbol of the once mighty Roman Empire which dominated so much of Europe and the Mediterranean basin for over 400 years.

A MONUMENT TO HADRIAN?

In 1783 two fragments of Roman inscriptions were discovered during restoration work at St Paul's Church, Jarrow (the site of Bede's monastery), on the south side of the Tyne. They are generally believed to have come from a large inscription recording the building of Hadrian's Wall, or perhaps its restoration under Septimius Severus. The size of the original panel from which the two fragments came can be estimated at 2m wide and 2.5m high. It can be argued that the inscription formed part of a large monument. Various possible locations have been suggested for the site of the monument, including at the mouth of the Tyne overlooking South Shields, on high ground in the vicinity of Jarrow overlooking the river, or even at Segedunum itself. As suggested in the reconstruction drawing on the cover, it may have been situated on the very end of the Branch Wall, literally the Wall's end. In such a location it would have formed an impressive monument to anyone arriving at the frontier from the sea.

Reconstruction of a monument to the victory of Hadrian's predecessor, Trajan, in Dacia (Romania). A similar monument may have been situated at Wallsend.
WB GRIFFITHS

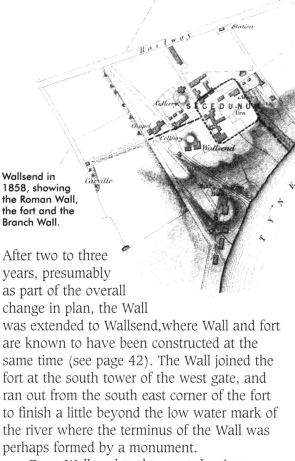

Wallsend in 1858, showing the Roman Wall, the fort and the Branch Wall.

After two to three years, presumably as part of the overall change in plan, the Wall was extended to Wallsend, where Wall and fort are known to have been constructed at the same time (see page 42). The Wall joined the fort at the south tower of the west gate, and ran out from the south east corner of the fort to finish a little beyond the low water mark of the river where the terminus of the Wall was perhaps formed by a monument.

From Wallsend to the coast the river becomes the frontier line. The decision to extend the Wall to Wallsend made good military sense as between them the forts at Wallsend and South Shields could watch over the river all the way to the coast. People today express surprise that the Wall did not run all the way to the coast, but to the Romans it was far more natural to use a river as a frontier than build an artificial barrier.

The Roman occupation of Hadrian's Wall

Shortly after Hadrian's death in AD 138 the Roman army advanced into Scotland, establishing a new frontier, the Antonine Wall, which was built of turf and timber. It was held for approximately 20 years before the army returned south to reoccupy Hadrian's Wall.

There was clearly trouble on the British frontier in the later second century AD. By the early third century the Emperor Septimius Severus arrived, with his two sons Caracalla (co-Emperor) and Geta, to campaign into Scotland. His expedition appears to have been a success, but he died in York in AD 211, and his two sons were more interested in who controlled the Empire than continuing the campaign. A peace was concluded with the northern tribes, and the army returned to the frontier line of Hadrian's Wall once more.

The third century appears to have been comparatively peaceful, but the fourth is once again marked by conflicts in the frontier zone. It should be pointed out that no archaeological evidence of such conflict has yet been discovered at Segedunum. Indeed much of what little we know of such conflicts comes from historical sources; there is little clear evidence on the ground for enemy action anywhere on Hadrian's Wall, with the exception of Arbeia fort at South Shields where a large section of the fort was burnt down.

Antonine Wall

Hadrian's Wall

Bust of Septimius Severus in the Museo Capitolino, Rome.

The fort of Segedunum

The fort model looking south.

Roman forts throughout the empire tended to follow a fairly regular plan, developed from the marching camps used by the Roman Republican army, and Segedunum is no exception. It is playing card shaped with a central range of buildings - headquarters (*principia*), commanding officer's house (*praetorium*), double granary (*horrea*), and a possible hospital (*valetudinarium*) - flanked to north and south by barracks, accommodation for the horses and men that made up the garrison of Segedunum. The buildings were enclosed within a defensive wall, in turn protected by a ditch system.

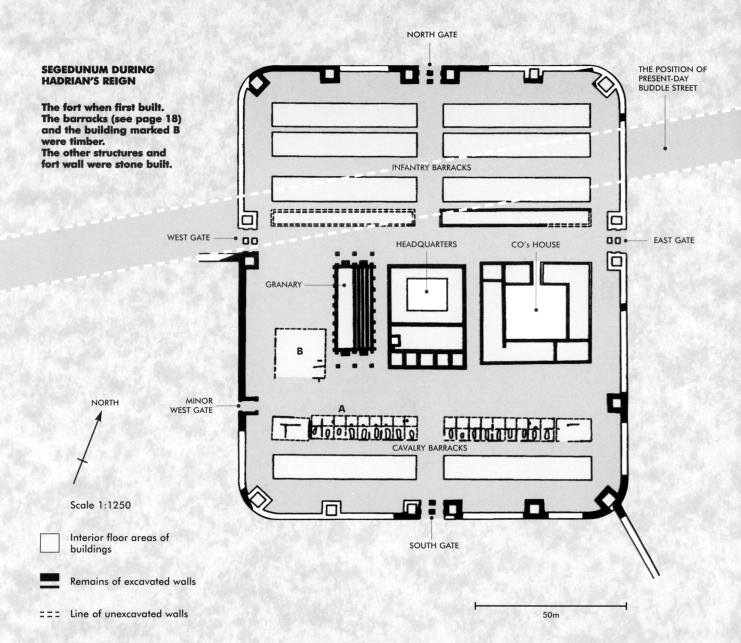

SEGEDUNUM DURING HADRIAN'S REIGN

The fort when first built.
The barracks (see page 18)
and the building marked B
were timber.
The other structures and
fort wall were stone built.

NORTH GATE

THE POSITION OF
PRESENT-DAY
BUDDLE STREET

INFANTRY BARRACKS

WEST GATE

EAST GATE

HEADQUARTERS

CO's HOUSE

GRANARY

B

NORTH

MINOR
WEST GATE

A

CAVALRY BARRACKS

Scale 1:1250

SOUTH GATE

Interior floor areas of
buildings

Remains of excavated walls

Line of unexcavated walls

50m

In common with other forts, Segedunum had a double portalled gate in each side, three of which opened out to land beyond Hadrian's Wall. In addition it also had a single portal gateway (the minor west gate or *porta quintana*), which lay on the west side of the fort to the south of Hadrian's Wall. Such 'extra' gates are a feature of forts on Hadrian's Wall, providing further access to the fort from a road running south of the Wall that linked the sites.

When first built much of the fort, in particular the barracks, appears to have been constructed in timber, although the defensive walls were of stone (see previous page for a plan of the fort as originally built in the Hadrianic period). However, in the mid-to-late second century AD, within about 50 years of the construction of the fort, all the buildings were rebuilt in stone, and some alterations made to the plan (see opposite), details of which are discussed in the descriptions of the individual buildings on pages 17-26.

Fort name and garrison

The name 'Segedunum' is believed to mean either 'strong' or 'victory' fort. It is recorded in a Roman document, the *Notitia Dignitatum*, written in the late fourth century AD, around the time of the end of Roman Britain.

Forts on Hadrian's Wall were usually occupied by single units, although at various periods separate, smaller units were sometimes added to a garrison. In the second century units were replaced at various times, but from the third century onwards units generally seem to have become more settled in their bases.

At Segedunum the garrison in the third and fourth centuries was the fourth cohort of Lingones, a mixed unit of 120 cavalry and 480 infantry. Originally raised in the province of *Germania Superior*, today part of eastern France, they probably came to Britain in the AD 70s as part of the initial Roman advance into the north.

During part of the second century Wallsend might have been held by the second cohort of Nervians, from *Gallia Belgica* (Belgium): a sculptural slab dedicated by the unit was found to the west of the fort.

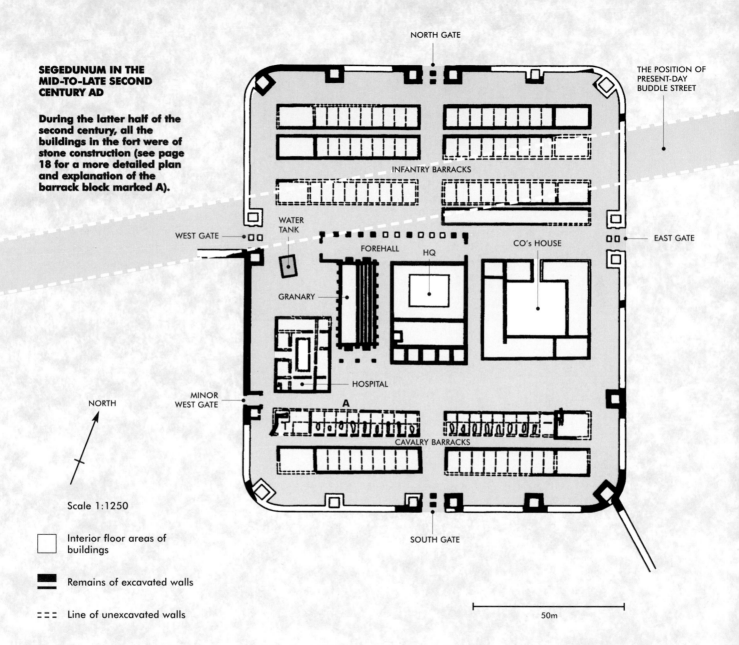

SEGEDUNUM IN THE MID-TO-LATE SECOND CENTURY AD

During the latter half of the second century, all the buildings in the fort were of stone construction (see page 18 for a more detailed plan and explanation of the barrack block marked A).

NORTH GATE

THE POSITION OF PRESENT-DAY BUDDLE STREET

INFANTRY BARRACKS

WEST GATE

WATER TANK

FOREHALL

HQ

CO's HOUSE

EAST GATE

GRANARY

HOSPITAL

A

MINOR WEST GATE

NORTH

CAVALRY BARRACKS

Scale 1:1250

SOUTH GATE

Interior floor areas of buildings

Remains of excavated walls

Line of unexcavated walls

50m

Commanders of the fort and their altars

Over the 300 years that Segedunum was garrisoned it would have had something like 100 different commanders; we know the names of four of them from inscriptions on altars found in the area. These altars were probably set up at religious and state festivals and their dedication would have been part of the regular duties of the commanding officer.

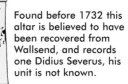

Found before 1732 this altar is believed to have been recovered from Wallsend, and records one Didius Severus, his unit is not known.

This altar was recovered from Tynemouth Priory in 1783. It too is to Jupiter and names Aelius Rufus as prefect of the Lingones. It was probably taken from the fort along with other blocks quarried from the site to help with building works at Tynemouth.
MUSEUM OF ANTIQUITIES, NEWCASTLE UPON TYNE

An altar to Jupiter found to the west of the fort was set up by Julius Honoratus. He describes himself as commanding the fourth Lingones, but also states that he was a centurion of the Second Legion Augusta, which was based at Caerleon in Wales. He was probably placed in temporary charge of the fort.
MUSEUM OF ANTIQUITIES, NEWCASTLE UPON TYNE

This facsimile of an altar to Jupiter was found near that of Honoratus to the west of the fort. It records Cornelius Celer as commanding officer of the Lingones.

We also know the name of one of the commanding officers of the Lingones in the second century, M. Statius Priscus, who went on to become Governor of several provinces, including Britain. However, we do not know where in Britain the unit was based when he was in command.

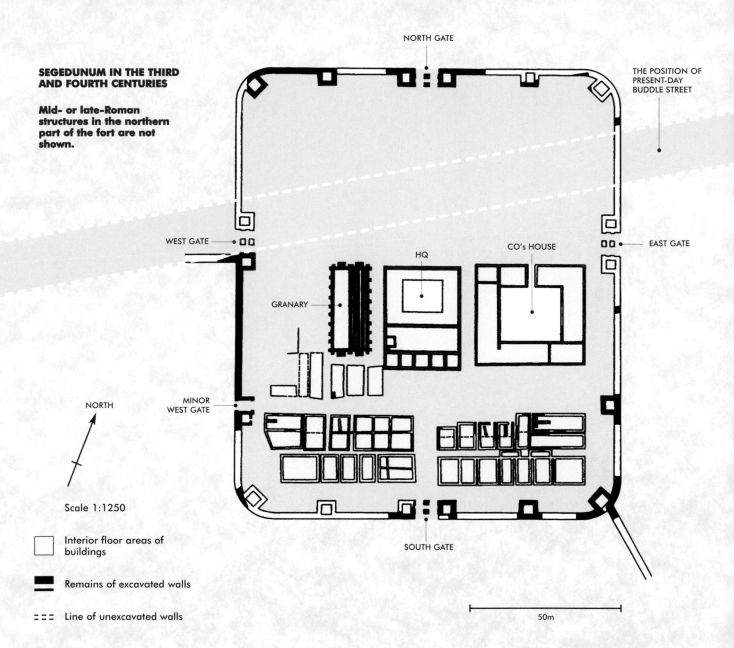

SEGEDUNUM IN THE THIRD AND FOURTH CENTURIES

Mid- or late-Roman structures in the northern part of the fort are not shown.

NORTH GATE

THE POSITION OF PRESENT-DAY BUDDLE STREET

WEST GATE

EAST GATE

HQ

CO's HOUSE

GRANARY

MINOR WEST GATE

NORTH

SOUTH GATE

Scale 1:1250

☐ Interior floor areas of buildings

■ Remains of excavated walls

≡≡≡ Line of unexcavated walls

50m

Buildings within the fort

The fort wall and gateways

The fort wall stood to a height of approximately 15 Roman feet, and was topped by a walkway with parapet wall. Outside the fort the wall presented a sheer face to any would-be attacker, but inside a turf rampart sloped down to ground level. Towers formed observation points at intervals around the wall.

At some point during the Roman period at least part of the fort wall near the minor west gate, the single portalled gate in the west wall, collapsed. This may be because a valley that ran parallel to the fort was being gradually eroded by a stream. A surviving section of the lowest course of the wall can be seen in this area, tilted slightly outwards.

Each of the four sides of the fort had a double gate with towers flanking the two portals. Stones from the east gate, excavated in 1912 and removed to Wallsend Park, have now been returned to their original position.

The minor west gate was the smallest gate in the fort, but was also the most used, as it provided the main access to the fort from the west. Excavations revealed that the road had been resurfaced on many occasions by the Romans. The gateway itself would have carried a tower above it. The building adjoining the south side of the gate may have allowed access to the chamber above the gate. However, at some point in the Roman period, this structure was demolished and the fort rampart extended over it.

Above: Remains of the east gate.

Left: The reconstructed gateway at Arbeia Roman fort in South Shields.

The barracks

There are ten barrack blocks within Segedunum fort. All were the subject of some excavation during the 1970s-80s, but this work generally concentrated on their later Roman levels. In 1997-8 the two barrack blocks immediately to the south of the central range were excavated in more detail. It was found that they followed the standard form for a Roman barrack, consisting of a series of pairs of rooms front and back with quarters for an officer at one end. In standard (infantry) barracks each pair of rooms would have been shared by eight men. The front room would have been used for the storage of equipment, while the rear room would have been used for sleeping. However, within each of the front rooms of the two excavated barracks a large pit covered by stone slabs was located, while hearths were generally found nearly exactly opposite them in the rear rooms (see plan below). Such an arrangement had been seen at several sites on the continent, but this excavation represented the first time a complete building plan with this distinctive layout had been recovered. It had been suggested by some continental excavators that such an arrangement may represent a barrack for cavalry troops, with the troops using the rear room, with their mounts stabled in the front, the pits being to collect the horses' urine. The barracks discovered at Segedunum serve to confirm this theory.

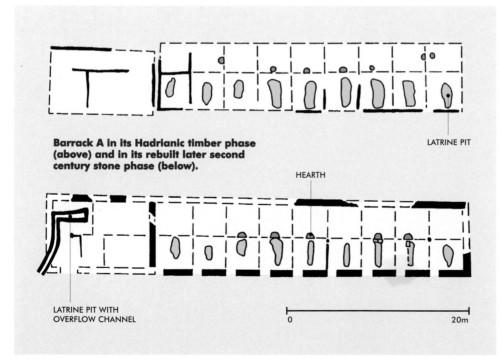

Barrack A in its Hadrianic timber phase (above) and in its rebuilt later second century stone phase (below).

LATRINE PIT

HEARTH

LATRINE PIT WITH
OVERFLOW CHANNEL

0   20m

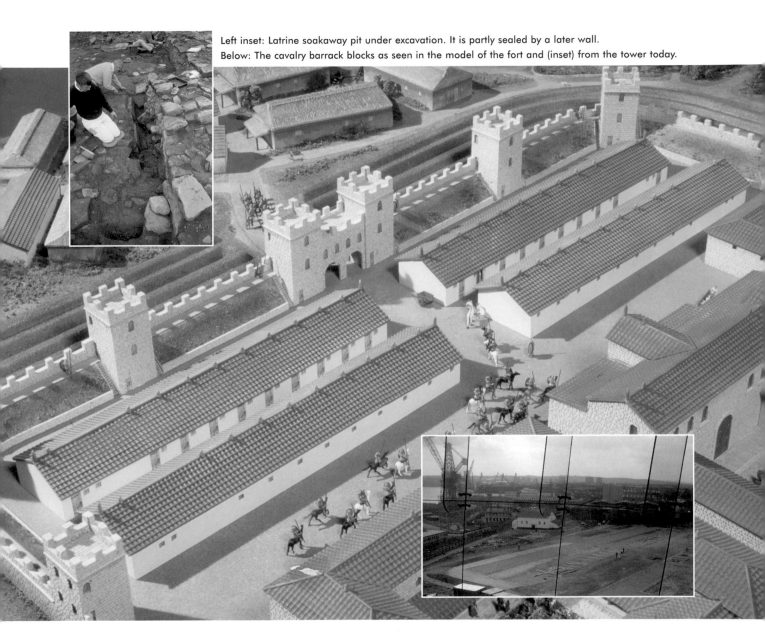

Left inset: Latrine soakaway pit under excavation. It is partly sealed by a later wall.

Below: The cavalry barrack blocks as seen in the model of the fort and (inset) from the tower today.

At first sight one surprising aspect of the latrine pits is that there are no channels to drain them away. In fact they operated as soakaway pits, and would occasionally have had lime added to neutralise the urine. However, the far more grandly constructed latrine pit seen in the officer's quarters of the western barrack was provided with an overflow channel, just in case!

To us it seems unhygienic to share a building with horses, but this is a view that has only evolved over the last century or so. The stable spaces (approximately 3.60m square) would be cramped by modern standards for the three horses that would have been kept in each. However, it should be remembered that Roman horses were smaller than modern ones, and there are parallels in the ancient world for the stabling of horses in spaces as narrow as this.

These cavalry barracks allowed the whole of the unit to be accommodated in the fort with its mounts, but of course for much of the time the horses would have been out on patrol, exercises, or being grazed outside the fort.

Reconstruction within the museum of a typical cavalry barrack interior, with a model in period costume adding a touch of authenticity.

Originally the two barracks were built in timber, but after 50 or so years they were rebuilt to the same plan in stone, but with timber internal partitions. It is assumed this was also the case for the other barracks within the fort. Further, if the two excavated examples are typical, it would appear that the barrack blocks were demolished in the third century and replaced by at least partially freestanding double room units (see plan page 15). This style of barrack accommodation has been seen in forts elsewhere on the northern frontier and may also represent cavalry barracks. Unfortunately these later Roman structures at Segedunum were poorly preserved as a result of damage done to the upper deposits in the fort by medieval ploughing and nineteenth century developments. However, remains of stone walls from these later structures have been consolidated for display on top of the fully laid out plans of the earlier cavalry barracks. This may appear confusing to the visitor, but serves to emphasise the fact that the layout of the fort did change through its 300 years of occupation.

The latrine in the stable block of the officers' quarters. Note the overflow channel at the bottom of the picture

BARRACKS

For more than 100 years archaeologists have been struggling to answer the question 'Where did they put the horses in Roman forts?' With the excavation of the two cavalry barracks at Segedunum the answer has been conclusively provided.

However, the excavations of the barracks also have a wider contribution to make to increasing our knowledge of the Roman army. We know that the garrison of Segedunum was a mixed unit of infantry and cavalry (*cohors equitata*). Such units are believed to have consisted of six centuries of infantry (a century consisting of around 80 men commanded by a centurion) and four *turmae* (with around 30 men in each commanded by a decurion) of cavalry. We know that two of the four barracks in the southern half of the fort were for cavalry, and it seems safe to assume that this was the case for all four, which would leave the six centuries of infantry in the six barracks in the northern section of the fort; that is to say that the cavalry were kept at one end of the fort and the infantry at the other. It can be suggested that this arrangement was standard throughout the Roman Empire, and as such this discovery represents a great leap forward in the understanding of the internal planning of Roman auxiliary forts.

A further breakthrough is that archaeologists can for the first time estimate how a cavalry *turma* was subdivided. The barracks at Wallsend were divided into nine pairs of rooms (*contubernia*). If we assume three men per *contubernium*, we have a strength of 27 men plus officer(s), a figure close to the 30 given by Roman writers for a *turma*.

Main image: The commanding officer's house.
Inset: The Headquarters building.

The commanding officer's house (*praetorium*)

The largest structure in the fort, much of this building was destroyed by cellars for Simpson's Hotel built in the early part of the twentieth century. However, it is clear that, in common with other such buildings in Roman forts, it had a central courtyard, and at some point in its life a bath-suite was added for the private use of the commander (*praefectus*), his family and guests. The commanding officer would have been the most important person in Wallsend, and the size of his house reflects this. Often unit commanders were from the upper echelons of society in the Mediterranean provinces of the Empire, and tended to move from appointment to appointment every few years, accompanied by their wives and family, and a retinue of servants.

Headquarters building (*principia*)

Situated at the centre of the fort, entry to the building was through an enclosed courtyard at the front surrounded on three sides by a covered walkway. In one corner of the courtyard is a water tank which would have supplied the water for religious ceremonies within the building. From the courtyard visitors would enter a large hall in which troops could be assembled to receive orders from the commanding officer. For such briefings the commander would stand on a 2m high platform (tribunal – not marked on site) at one end of the hall. This lay at the opposite end from a door which provided access to the commanding officer's house. The stone threshold slab for this door, worn with the passage of time, can still be seen on the site. The

The steps down into the strongroom, formed from stones originally used elsewhere in the fort.

door allowed the commander to make his entrance and exit through his men at the start and conclusion of any gathering.

At the rear of the building was a set of five rooms each opening onto the hall. These contained various offices. The most significant was the central room. This contained a strongroom set into the ground, used for the storage of the garrison's funds. Above it was a shrine (*aedes*) that contained the standards of the unit. The centre of the fort, these two rooms were guarded night and day. The stones used to form the steps into the strongroom can clearly be seen to have been reused from another structure.

Forehall

This structure was built at the end of the second century, originally in timber, but soon replaced in stone. It was a large, tall building, the walls of which were formed by a series of piers constructed from stone blocks (the position of the bases for these piers are marked out on site by large squares). The spaces between the piers were then infilled with stone walls. Archaeologists are not certain as to the use of the hall, but it may have been used for parades or ceremonial gatherings. Associated with this structure is the blocking off of the south end of the road that ran between the east side of the double granary and the west side of the headquarters building.

Double granary (*horrea*)

This building was used to store the supplies for the garrison. Most forts had a pair of granaries, and this building is two granaries joined together. Two features make granary foundations easy for archaeologists to identify. The first are the buttressed external walls. These were necessary to provide support to the walls which carried a heavy roof and louvres to aid ventilation. The second can be seen in the eastern half of the granary where 'sleeper' walls have been built to support a raised floor. Raised floors were a vital feature of the granaries as they allowed air to circulate beneath the stores, thus reducing damp, and made it harder for rodents to get at the supplies. The doors at each end had projecting roofs supported on columns (porticos) so that supplies could be kept dry when being unloaded.

As with all the buildings in the fort the granary went through several alterations during its life, including the demolition of the northern portico to allow the construction of the forehall, and the construction of a small building against its north-west corner, the

purpose of which is unknown, but perhaps could have been added for a clerk in charge of supplies.

The water tank during excavation.

Water tank

The water tank appears to have been added to the fort in the early third century. It could well have been supplied by a small aqueduct bringing water from one of the small springs known to have existed to the west of the fort. The tank would have been used to allow sediment in the water to settle before the water was distributed around the fort. At some point what appears to be an overflow was added; it carried water down through the hospital to allow for the flushing of the latrines there.

Hospital (*valetudinarium*)

The first building on this site was of timber, but little survives of its plan. The stone building that has been laid out for display was built in the AD 160s. It originally consisted of four ranges of rooms built around a central courtyard with covered walkway, or veranda. Such a plan resembles a scaled down version of the commanding officer's house; however, when seen in forts, buildings of this plan are usually identified as hospitals.

We have no proof that it was used as a hospital, but the room in the south west corner was a large latrine, indicating that the building was used by several people, rather than being the home of an officer. The other

Remains of a stone toilet seat found re-used in a drain in the hospital toilet.

rooms could have been used for wards, while the shaded courtyard would have been a quiet area for recuperating soldiers. Another possible suggestion for the function of this type of building is that it may have been a workshop, but no evidence of any industrial processes was recovered from it, so it seems most likely that it would indeed have functioned as a hospital.

The hospital.

In the third century the east range of the hospital was demolished to create a wider roadway between it and the granary. Subsequently the whole building was demolished, and replaced by a series of freestanding timber structures, most likely used as a barrack block (see plan, page 15). The positions of these structures have not been marked out on the site, but the east wall of the hospital does show damage where it was cut through by the digging of post holes for the upright timbers of these buildings.

Post holes cut into the hospital wall.

MEDICAL CARE IN ROMAN FORTS

Although lacking anything like the medical knowledge we have today, the Roman Army well understood that it had to keep its men fit for duty. Each legion had its own medical staff, specialists in various areas, and a hospital within the walls of its fortress. It seems clear that each auxiliary unit would have had at least a doctor (*medicus*) and some assistants, either qualified or drawn from the ranks and trained. Several texts survive from the Roman period giving detailed accounts of the treatment for various illnesses and injuries.

The communal toilets in the recontructed bath-house. Those in the hospital would have looked very similar.
LM KAY

Outside the fort

A civilian settlement (*vicus*) sprang up to the south and west of the fort to accommodate traders and craftsmen supplying the garrison. Little is known of the settlement, but it is clear that it extended down to the river, and almost certainly would have included some sort of harbour facility for the offloading of supplies. Discoveries in the early nineteenth century suggest that the bath-house at Segedunum lay at the bottom of the hill near the river, where the 'Ship In the Hole' public house now stands. The settlement seems to have had a defensive bank and ditch on its west side (as shown on the illustration on the cover). It was enclosed to the north and east by the fort and Branch Wall (the section of Hadrian's Wall running from the fort to the river). Study of the finds from limited excavations in the civilian settlement indicate that, in common with similar sites on Hadrian's Wall, it was largely abandoned by the fourth century AD, a hundred years before the collapse of Roman Britain.

The civilian settlement south of Segedunum as depicted in the museum's fort model.

To the north of the fort, beyond Hadrian's Wall, traces of field systems in use during the third century AD have been excavated. To the west, on the road from Segedunum towards *Pons Aelius* (the Roman fort at Newcastle) there may have been a temple complex and cemetery. Several altars and a dedication stone, making reference in particular to Mercury, the Roman god of traders and merchants, were found there during the laying out of allotments at the end of the nineteenth century.

Hadrian's Wall

An 80m length of Hadrian's Wall has been excavated at Wallsend, showing the potential for its preservation beneath the rest of urban Tyneside. To the north of the Wall was a ditch, the south edge of which is marked by a slight ridge in the grass. Unfortunately the close proximity of a modern street made it impossible to excavate the ditch for display. Between the ditch and the

Fragment of relief, probably of the goddess Diana, showing a hunting dog at her feet. Found in rubble from the collapse of a repair to a section of the Wall.

Wall were found a series of post-holes, now marked by upright timbers. These were the position of an extra defence for the Wall. They probably formed a type of natural entanglement.The posts appear to have been in use around the end of the second century AD.

Running south from Hadrian's Wall was a series of ditches and an earth bank that formed, along with the posts, part of the defences of either the civilian settlement or an annexe to the fort. None of these features are visible on the site today.

CIPPI

On occasion the Roman army would add extra defences beyond the walls of its camps. Traces of such features, which vary from barbed iron spikes to sharpened stakes hidden in pits, have been seen at various sites throughout the Roman world.

However, the discovery of the post-holes at Wallsend marks the first time such extra defences have been seen by archaeologists on Hadrian's Wall. The post-holes are arranged in a staggered formation which resembles Caesar's description of defensive works employed by him at the siege of Alesia in France, where branches with sharpened ends (*cippi*) were set to form an entanglement that would create an obstacle to attackers similar to the role a barbed wire fence would play today.

Post holes for *cippi* as seen during the excavation.

Hadrian's Wall under excavation. The central section shows how the Wall has shifted to the south down the valley.

The large blocks of stone used to repair the Wall, lying where they fell after the collapse of the south face.

At the west end of the site is a spectacular section of Hadrian's Wall. At this point the Wall had to cross the head of a small valley. This valley was filled in after the Roman period, thus preserving the remains of the south side of the Wall which stands eight courses high, quite exceptional survival given that it had lain undiscovered beneath a busy town for years.

This section of Wall also clearly shows several episodes of collapse and repair. On the east side of the valley the north face can be seen where it has collapsed back on itself as the Wall slipped southwards down the valley. After this the Romans rebuilt the Wall. The new north face has not survived, but the repair to the south face consists of large blocks of stones, including a reused window head, taken from another building, possibly a tower or gateway of the fort.

Further to the west the Wall can be seen to have undergone several episodes of collapse and repair in the Roman period.

There can be no doubt that this section of wall, representing as it does the first clear evidence for repairs being made to the Wall in the late Roman period, is an impressive discovery. Given that so little of the Wall line has been excavated beneath the rest of urban Tyneside it also suggests that other such discoveries may well be waiting to be made beneath the streets and houses.

Top: Large blocks forming a repair to the south side of Hadrian's Wall.

Above: The north face of Hadrian's Wall, showing its collapse to the south.

Right: A segment of stone window head arch, re-used in a repair to the south face of the Wall.

Branch Wall

Hadrian's Wall ran from the south-east corner of the fort down to the river Tyne, literally the Wall's end! Remains of the Wall may still survive beneath the shipyard today.

Excavations in 2000 revealed the foundations of the Wall following a steep slope to the river immediately to the south of the National trail/cycleway to the south of the fort. As with the section of Hadrian's Wall just described, there is evidence for repair and rebuilding on this section of the Wall.

A section of the Branch Wall (the length of Hadrian's Wall that ran from the fort to the river) was found in 1903 during excavations to enlarge Swan Hunter shipyard in advance of the construction of the Mauretania.

The Branch Wall returned to the site.

At the time of its discovery it was hoped that the section of Wall could be left on view in the shipyard. Unfortunately this proved impractical, and instead the Wall was removed to Wallsend Park about two-thirds of a mile north of the fort. It was joined there in 1912 by stones removed from the site of the east gateway of the fort.

The Wall stones were moved at least once within the park before being returned to the site in 1991. Unlike the east gate however, the stones from the Wall have not been returned to their original position, which is today marked by a plaque in the shipyard. Instead they have been assembled on the line of the Branch Wall between the site of Segedunum and the route of the Hadrian's Wall trail.

The Branch Wall in Wallsend Park in the 1930s.

After the Romans

By the beginning of the fifth century AD the Roman Empire in western Europe was slowly disintegrating because of a combination of internal problems such as an increasingly unwieldy administrative system, and incursions of barbarians from north of the Rhine and Danube hungry for land. In AD 409 the Emperor Honorius effectively abandoned Britain to its fate. This is not to say that the Romans left, just that the structure of society slowly collapsed due to the lack of an organised core. Gradually the people living at Wallsend would have had to become ever more self sufficient.

There is no firm evidence for what happened in Wallsend during the next few centuries. However, although the later levels of the fort were much disturbed by post-medieval activity, a few artefacts hint at Anglo-Saxon occupation in the vicinity, including the possibility of a cemetery.

By the time of the Norman Conquest it would appear that the settlement had moved inland about half a mile from the area of the fort to the site of Wallsend Green today.

Anglian copper alloy strap end.

This move may have been prompted by fear of raiders sailing up the Tyne.

It is interesting to note that even as early as the eleventh century the settlement was called 'Wallesende', showing that the inhabitants had not forgotten the origin of their town. After the settlement moved north the site of the fort remained undeveloped until the late eighteenth century. One antiquarian, John Horsley, writing in the early eighteenth century, describes it as follows: 'The ruins of a Roman Station and town at this place are still very discernible; tho' it has all been plowed, and is now a very rich meadow...'.

Wallsend Colliery

In the mid-eighteenth century this area of Wallsend was owned by the Dean and Chapter of Durham, and in 1777 they leased the mineral rights to William Chapman who set out to mine coal. After a first exploratory shaft was lost to quick-sand he began to sink another shaft (later to become the A pit) immediately to the west of the fort, a little to the south of the west gate. Unfortunately the loan taken out to finance the work was recalled in 1780, and the project was taken over by William Russell, one of the creditors.

Russell's gamble paid off: in 1781 the High Main coal seam was struck at a depth of 666 feet (around 200m). Almost immediately a second shaft (Wallsend B pit) was sunk 70 metres to the north of the first, adjacent to the north-west corner of the fort. Remains associated with this shaft can be seen on the site today.

The site of the fort in the mid nineteenth century looking towards Newcastle. Painted c.1848 by Henry Richardson.
LAING ART GALLERY

Wallsend A pit in the early nineteenth century, by Thomas Hair.

By the beginning of the nineteenth century Wallsend Colliery consisted of six interconnected shafts spread throughout the township and produced the highest quality household coal in the world. As such it carried a high price and was very much in demand. The coal was moved from the shafts on waggonways to collier ships waiting on the Tyne next to the site of the fort. From here the coal was shipped, primarily to London.

The fame of the colliery brought several important visitors to Wallsend, including, on 13th December 1816, Grand Duke Nicholas of Russia. Standing at the top of one of the shafts he likened it to "the mouth of Hell" and could not be persuaded to descend into the mine to continue the tour.

The great success of Wallsend Colliery was largely due to the skill of its viewers (managers) especially John Buddle Junior. Buddle succeeded his father as viewer of Wallsend in 1803. He was the leading expert on coal mining in the early nineteenth century, and made many improvements in the working of coal mines, particularly in terms of safety.
LAING ART GALLERY

In 1820-21 a deeper seam (the Bensham seam) was encountered at 870 feet (around 265m). By 1831 the High Main seam was worked out and the B pit effectively stopped functioning, acting predominantly as an air shaft for the workings.

1835 saw a great tragedy at the colliery. At about 2pm on Thursday 18th June a large underground blast occurred. Of 107 men and boys (32 of whom were children aged 8-14) and ten horses underground, only four men and a boy survived. The most poignant discovery was of the bodies of 17 young boys who had been overcome by the fumes along with one of the deputy overmen of the colliery who had been leading them out, believing they were only 300 metres from safety. In fact the G pit shaft they had been attempting to reach had been blocked by the explosion.

By the mid-nineteenth century the colliery had closed as a result of flooding. It reopened in the 1890s, but the main workings were located around half a mile to the north of the site of the fort. By the end of the century the A pit shaft was gone. The B pit shaft operated as an air shaft for Wallsend Colliery (later known as the Rising Sun pit) until its final closure in 1969.

WAGGONWAYS

One of the reasons that Wallsend Colliery and others in the area were successful, apart from the quality of their coal, was their ease of access to the river. Coal was loaded into waggons which were then hauled on rails (at first by horses, but later by steam locomotives) down to the river where the coal was transferred into ships for transportation to London and beyond. These waggonways criss-crossed the landscape around the fort, their routes often changing, in particular in relation to the A and B pits. Quite a few of the modern roads in the area began life as waggonways, including Buddle Street, the road which runs across the fort, and Benton Way, which runs down to the river to the west of the excavated section of Hadrian's Wall. One of the earliest steam locomotives developed for hauling coal waggons was in use at Wallsend.

Coal staiths at Wallsend, by Thomas Hair.

The colliery remains

Excavation of the colliery site was limited for the most part to the clearance of demolition material to reveal the structures that can be seen on site. The remains of the colliery were better preserved than had been thought.

Originally the archaeologists were excavating to locate the remains of the ditch in front of Hadrian's Wall, but soon changed tactics once the extent of the preservation of the colliery became apparent.

The shaft itself is sealed by a concrete cap. To the south the remains of brick and stone structures have been conserved. Those seen in a hollow are original remains, but the structures on higher ground have been reburied, their positions being marked out in brick.

The large circular brick structures are the bases for boilers. A fire would be lit in the base of the structure to heat a boiler situated above. This would create steam power which was used for pumping water from the mine and for the lifting of coal and men.

The stone walls on the site were the foundations for the massive engines that the boilers powered. The small circles of brick mark the position of ventilation 'tubes' used to draw foul air away from the main shaft and help in the ventilation of the mine.

For the most part the remains that are visible are of the late eighteenth and early nineteenth centuries, although the features to the north of the shaft belong to a later period.

Shipbuilding

Although the coal mining industry was in decline in Wallsend by the mid-nineteenth century, other industries were growing that more than made up for the loss. Nearby chemical works were being developed, but at the site of the fort shipbuilding became the dominant activity.

Launched in 1906 from the Swan Hunter shipyard the *Mauretania* was the largest passenger ship ever built on the Tyne. She could carry over 2,000 passengers, and carried a crew of 812. In her day she was famous on both sides of the Atlantic, and held the Blue Riband for the fastest crossing of the ocean from 1910 to 1929. During World War I she operated as a troopship, and a hospital ship during the Gallipoli campaign. She was finally broken up in 1935.

World Unicorn supertanker towering over the terraced houses that used to stand on the site of the fort.
NEWCASTLE CHRONICLE & JOURNAL

THE RIVER TYNE

Throughout the last 2000 years, the river has been the most significant character in Wallsend's story. Hadrian finished his Wall here because the river was sufficient to act as frontier to the coast. After the Roman period it was the threat the Tyne posed as a convenient route for attackers that caused the people of Wallsend to move inland. Once coal mining began, the river had a vital role in allowing the valuable commodity to be transported easily to distant markets, and it is self evident that without the river there could have been no shipbuilding industry. Throughout this time the river has followed broadly the same route, although the last 200 years have seen much artificial narrowing of the Tyne and deepening of its channel to allow ever larger vessels to navigate it.

Workers leaving the *Mauretania*. This image gives some idea of the vast numbers employed in the shipyards during this time.

In the 1840s iron shipbuilding came to the Tyne. Although revolutionary, the industry was slow to develop by today's standards. Nevertheless it gradually spread and in 1863 a shipyard was opened on the north bank of the Tyne adjacent to the Roman fort. The firm, Schlesinger, Davies and Co., was very successful for 21 years, but never recovered from a shipbuilding recession in 1884 and by 1893 it closed.

In 1873 another yard opened immediately to the east of Schlesinger, Davies & Co. After a rocky start, Charles Sheriton Swan was made manager and the yard prospered under the new name of C. S. Swan & Co. However, in 1879 tragedy struck when Swan fell off the bow of a Dover to Calais Steamer and was killed. Swan's wife sought a new partner for the firm and in 1880 George Burton Hunter of Sunderland became Managing Director.

Launch of HMS *Richmond* from Swan Hunter, 1993.
WB GRIFFITHS

Gradually the yard grew. In 1875 C. S. Swan and Hunter became a limited company. The yard now occupied an area of 23 acres and continued to grow. In 1897 the vacant site of Schlesinger, Davies and Co., to the south of Segedunum fort, was incorporated into the yard.

In the 1880s, in response to the need for housing for the workers flooding into Wallsend to work in the heavy industries, a builder acquired the site of the fort. It soon disappeared under a series of streets, destined to remain hidden from view for almost 100 years. In June 1903 the yards of C. S. Swan and Hunter Ltd. and J. Wigham Richardson at Low Walker merged to bid for the order to build the *Mauretania*, the Tyne's most famous passenger liner. This amalgamation was to prove permanent and brought the two yards together in a highly successful association under the name Swan, Hunter & Wigham Richardson Ltd.

Swan Hunter became one of the world's premier shipbulders, building over 1,600 vessels for world-wide destinations during its 130 year life span, including oil tankers, ice breakers, destroyers, submarines, cargo liners and floating docks.

Today, despite industry-wide recession, Swan Hunter is still a dominent feature of the landscape of Wallsend. Now owned by a Dutch firm, the yard is determined to reclaim its place on the world stage.

Launched in 1903 from Swan Hunter the *Carpathia* gained fame as the ship which rescued the survivors from the sinking of the *Titanic* in 1912, her radio operator receiving the distress call just as he was preparing for bed. The *Carpathia* herself sank with the loss of five crewmen after being torpedoed by German submarine *U55* on July 17th 1918.
TYNE & WEAR ARCHIVES

Archaeology

At the end of the nineteenth century the science of archaeology was still very much in its infancy. Across the river at South Shields pioneering work had been undertaken to excavate and display a part of the Roman fort there. Unfortunately Wallsend was not so well served. Some limited excavations were carried out by A.S. Stevenson on behalf of the Society of Antiquaries of Newcastle upon Tyne, but no detailed results were ever published. There was a final effort to preserve the south east corner of the fort as a small park. An attempt was made to establish a public subscription to raise the £680 required to buy the land, but it was not successful and the entire fort was gradually buried beneath terraced housing.

1929 archaeologist's tunnel under Buddle street along the north face of Hadrian's Wall. The south side of the west gate can be seen in the background.

By the beginning of the twentieth century the site was watched over by Walter Corder, a local chemical manufacturer and amateur antiquarian, who recorded the discovery of a section of Hadrian's Wall running down to the river in 1903; it was he who excavated the site of the east gate of the fort in advance of its site being obliterated by Simpson's Hotel which was constructed in 1912. The remains of both the Wall and the east gate were removed to Wallsend Park following their discovery, but have now been returned and incorporated into the display of the site.

In 1929, as part of a major campaign of excavations on the eastern end of Hadrian's Wall to provide information for a chapter in the monumental *Northumberland County History* series of volumes, the great Wall scholar F.G. Simpson carried out a number of small scale digs in and around the fort. For the most part, these consisted of small trenches designed to locate the exact position of the fort and Hadrian's Wall. They also included a closer study of the north gate, as well as the cutting of a tunnel (see illustration on previous page) under Buddle Street, the road which cuts the fort in two, along the north face of Hadrian's Wall to its junction with the south side of the west gate of the fort. This excavation was of great significance as it revealed that fort and Wall were built at the same time, and Simpson concluded that the whole section

Above: Statue of the goddess Fortuna, found in the commanding officer's house at Segedunum.

Left: Excavations in the north east corner of the fort in 1975.

Right: Segedunum from the air, May 2001.
D J WOOLLISCROFT, UNIVERSITY OF MANCHESTER.

351

383

362

355

361

340

352 *Shaft*

365

363

SEGEDUNUM
(*Site of*)

363

Wes: Meth: Chap:

W a l l

Shafts

L a w s

Wallsend Colliery

or

W E L L WAY

L a w s

346

34

ROMAN
REMAINS
found here

345

of Wall from Newcastle to Wallsend was part of an addition to the original plan which, he suggested, saw the Wall terminating at Newcastle.

In the 1970s the, by now run-down, terraced housing over the fort was cleared in preparation for the construction of new housing. In advance of this, rescue excavations commenced in 1975 in the northern part of the fort under the direction of the late Charles Daniels of the Department of

Archaeology, Newcastle University. At the time it was assumed that much of the fort had been destroyed by the building of the houses in the 1880s, but in fact the excavations showed the site to be far better preserved than anyone had previously hoped.

North Tyneside Council, in what was for the time a far sighted decision, agreed that the remains were too significant to be built over and instead felt that the site should be preserved for the future. The rescue excavations became research excavations and continued until 1984. The particular achievement of this series of excavations was that almost the complete plan of the fort was recovered, showing its development over the 300 years of its occupation by the Roman army. No other fort on Hadrian's Wall has been anything like as fully excavated.

Following this work the site of the fort was grassed over with just the headquarters

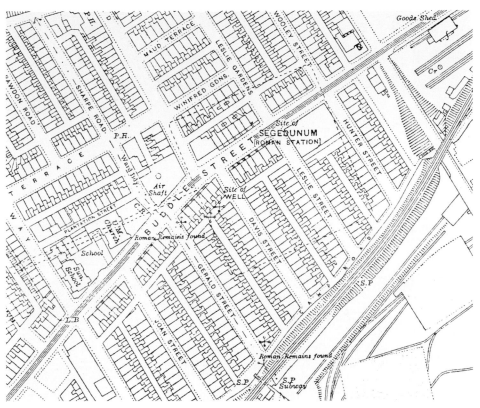

building (*principia*) at the centre of the fort left on display. The fort defences were marked out in modern paving and a small museum, the Wallsend Heritage Centre, was opened to the north of the site. Over the next ten years several small scale excavations were conducted outside the fort by Tyne and Wear Museums Department of Archaeology, and a section of Hadrian's Wall was reconstructed.

In 1996 North Tyneside Council was successful in attracting funding to develop Segedunum as a large new visitor attraction. As part of the development Tyne and Wear Museums Archaeology Department conducted a major new series of excavations. These included two cavalry barracks, the granary, hospital and quintan gate in the fort, as well as 80m of Hadrian's Wall to the west of the reconstruction, and the site of the Wallsend B pit. In addition, the sites of the bath-house and the new entrance block of the museum had to

be excavated before any building work commenced, in order to ensure that the development would not be damaging any part of Wallsend's heritage. Excavation of the entrance block revealed an extra ditch further from the fort than predicted, which led to the replanning of the design of this section of the museum to avoid damage to the archaeology of the site. All these excavations form the backbone of the interpretation and display of the site today.

Once excavation works were completed the ground plan of the fort was laid out, making Segedunum almost the only place in the whole of the Roman Empire where visitors can see a fort plan laid out in

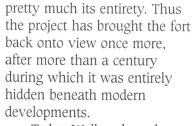

pretty much its entirety. Thus the project has brought the fort back onto view once more, after more than a century during which it was entirely hidden beneath modern developments.

Today Wallsend can lay claim to being one of the most extensively excavated forts in the Roman Empire, and certainly to being one of the most comprehensively understood on Hadrian's Wall. However, this is not the same as saying that all the remains in the fort were excavated. Archaeology is a detailed process and at Wallsend, as at all the other forts on Hadrian's Wall, much work remains to be done. Many archaeological deposits within the fort remain unexcavated and there are doubtless many more surprises waiting beneath the ground at Segedunum to confound and astonish us all.

Right: Looking east along Buddle Street at excavation work during 1975.

Below: Roman shrine, made of lead, found in a cavalry barrack at Segedunum.

Present day

The fort of Segedunum today lies at the heart of urban industrial Tyneside, a setting in marked contrast to that of other Roman museums along Hadrian's Wall. Indeed, this was one of the reasons for the development of Segedunum as a visitor attraction, as it highlighted the way in which landscapes can change through time, in a way that is not possible elsewhere on this World Heritage Site.

The development of Segedunum cost a total of £9 million, and took from January 1997 to June 2000 to complete. Many people took a hand in the work including, at one point, over 100 people on the archaeological excavations alone. The site is made up of a number of different components designed to provide the visitor with an idea of life at Roman Segedunum, and also with an understanding of the way the area has changed over the past 2000 years.

The Museum

The museum building was originally built in 1943 and operated as the canteen for Swan Hunter. Today it contains two floors of displays. The ground floor includes an area which tells of the methods archaeologists have used to learn about the site over the years. The rest of the level contains displays illustrating what life was like in the fort. At the centre is a mock up of the courtyard of the headquarters building at the centre of the fort, which includes a detailed model of the fort. Other displays include reconstructions of the inside of a pair of rooms in a cavalry barrack, the commanding officer's

house, a granary and hospital. In addition you can hear from Roman inhabitants of the fort about life at Segedunum. The displays also include Roman artefacts found during the excavations on the site.

Upstairs are displays about coal-mining and shipbuilding, as well as a temporary display gallery, where a variety of exhibitions are mounted. You can also visit the film theatre where an audio-visual presentation outlines the history of Wallsend over the past 2000 years.

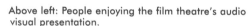

Above left: People enjoying the film theatre's audio visual presentation.

Above right: The Stratigraphic display within the museum, which demonstrates how layers of archaeological finds can build up over the centuries.

Left: Roman horse harness fitting. The owner's name is punched into it.

Main picture right: The fort model at the centre of the Roman Gallery.

Inset right: What is now the Roman Gallery in the museum, before its conversion.

The viewing tower

The tower is 34m high in total and provides excellent views over much of the surrounding area.
In particular there is the view over the fort site in which the positions of the buildings as they were around AD 200 have been marked out. Displays in the tower show computer models of the landscape at various stages over the past 2000 years, demonstrating how the site has developed and changed.
Designed by North Tyneside Council's Building Design Agency, the tower can accommodate 50 visitors at a time. The form of the tower is intended to evoke the architectural styles and engineering of the shipyards of the Tyne, but also stands as a visibly modern structure, as befitting a museum opened at the start of the twenty-first century.

Left: The viewing tower provides the ideal viewpoint for seeing the layout of the fort - and also of the surrrounding district.

Right: The viewing tower as seen from the reconstructed section of Hadrian's Wall and as seen from a cavalry barrack in the fort.

The reconstructed bath-house

The reconstructed bath-house lies to the south of the fort in the area of the civilian settlement (*vicus*) which spread from the fort to the river. The site was excavated before construction work began, and traces of rectangular houses, with both stone and timber foundations were located, indicating that the area had been built upon in the Roman period. However, very little survived, much of the remains having been destroyed by ploughing in the medieval period. The site of the original bath-house at Segedunum is not known for certain, although records of discoveries made in the early nineteenth century would seem to indicate that it lay further down the hill towards the river, in the area occupied by the 'Ship in the Hole' public house today.

This inscription was found in the area of the quintan gate during excavations in 1998, and would have formed one edge of a panel recording the rebuilding of a structure around the start of the third century AD. The first two lines probably listed the official Imperial titles, while the fourth can be reconstructed as A SOLO, a term used to indicate rebuilding. It is the third line which gives the title of the building in question, BALI - which can be read as *balineum*, or bath-house. So the archaeologists managed to find proof of a bath-house at Segedunum while builders were already working on the reconstruction.

The reconstructed bath-house is based on the impressive surviving remains of the bath-house at Chesters Roman fort on Hadrian's Wall, but has been laid out in mirror image in order to fit the space available for it. Chesters is one of the best preserved Roman buildings in the country, with walls surviving to an average height of two metres. Nevertheless, even with this excellent starting point a great deal of research had to take place before the exact form of the reconstruction could be decided upon. This involved the architects and archaeologists working closely together to sift the mass of information from similar sites throughout the Roman Empire. The finished reconstruction represents this work and gives a fine impression of how the bath-house at Segedunum may have appeared.

Cut-away floor in the bath-house which demonstrates the roman method of under-floor heating.

The visitor enters the changing room, a huge space that could have functioned as a place for both political and social gatherings within the *vicus*. From here the Roman bather would have progressed through a series of cold, warm and hot rooms, in a manner similar to a modern Turkish bath. In the cold room (*frigidarium*) was a plunge bath in which the bather could freshen up at the start of his bath, or cool down after having been in the heated rooms. Next was the warm room (*tepidarium*) in which the bather could be anointed with oils. In the hot room (*caldarium*) was a hot bath as well as a small fountain (*labrum*). Temperature and humidity were high in this room, and bathers would not stay for too long before moving back to one of the warm rooms. Skin would be scraped with a *strigil* to remove ingrained dirt, and the bather could also choose to have a massage.

BATHS IN THE ROMAN WORLD

Roman baths are today seen as one of the great symbols of the civilised sophistication of life in the Roman Empire. Several large bath-houses were built in Rome capable of accommodating hundreds of bathers at a time. Every city and town would have had its own baths, and certainly every fort on Hadrian's Wall was equipped with one similar to the example reconstructed at Segedunum.

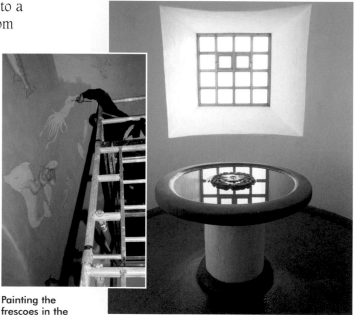

Painting the frescoes in the baths.

The *labrum*, a small fountain, in the hot room.
GRAEME PEACOCK

54

Segedunum fort site

The positions of all the buildings in the fort have been laid out, showing the ground plan of Segedunum as it would have been around AD 200. In places where the recent excavations revealed original Roman stonework it has been consolidated and displayed. However, in those areas from which the stone was 'robbed away', or where there has been no recent excavation, the positions of the buildings are marked out using pin kerbs and cobbles. Yellow gravel marks internal rooms.

WHERE DID ALL THE STONE GO?

Following the abandonment of the fort most of the stone used in the building of Segedunum was removed from the site over the centuries to construct buildings elsewhere such as Tynemouth Priory. In effect the fort became a convenient quarry. In some cases the only evidence left to archaeologists for the position of a wall is the trench left behind once the stone had been removed.

Hadrian's Wall: the reconstruction

The reconstructed section of Wall was built between 1993-96 and opened in 1997. It is positioned immediately to the south of the exposed foundations of the original Wall in order to remind people that much about its form is conjectural. It stands 12 Roman feet (3.5m) high to the level of the wall walk, which is the lowest generally accepted height for Hadrian's Wall; in fact it could have been as much as three Roman feet (0.885 metres) higher. We do not know what the top of Hadrian's Wall looked like, but most people believe it included a walkway, which means a parapet wall of the type shown on the reconstruction would have been needed to provide the soldiers with protection.

Roman throwing stones, found at Segedunum. They would have been thrown at attackers.

The reconstructed wall undergoing finishing touches.

Was Hadrian's Wall decorated?

The Romans did not generally appreciate the look of natural stone, and often plastered it over, sometimes even going to the trouble of picking out false joints in the plaster and painting them red. This would have the effect of giving a rough stone wall the appearance of having been constructed from perfectly dressed squared off blocks.

Excavations on the central section of Hadrian's Wall near Housesteads Roman Fort in the mid 1980s found some evidence to suggest that the Wall may have been painted with whitewash. An excavation at Denton, on the west side of Newcastle, found evidence for a plastered surface, with lines emphasising the joints between the stones. No evidence for decoration of the Wall has been seen at Segedunum, but this does not necessarily mean that none existed; such decoration could simply have weathered away over the years.

Part of the reconstruction has been decorated in a variety of styles to show how the Romans could have decorated the wall. Visitors are invited to make up their own mind!

Other sites to visit

A wide variety of sites concerned with the Roman remains on Hadrian's Wall can be found along its entire length. All are fully listed in the variety of guide books available concerning the Wall. Within urban Tyneside there are two sites particularly worth visiting:

Arbeia Roman Fort – South Shields

This began life as a regular fort, but was altered to become a supply base in the early third century AD. A significant portion of the fort has been excavated and consolidated for visitors. The south west gateway has been impressively reconstructed, and further reconstructions of a barrack and part of the commanding officer's house are in progress. There is an excellent small museum displaying artefacts from the site as well as the Timequest gallery where visitors can try

Re-enactment of a Roman religious ceremony at Arbeia Roman Fort

their hand at some of the techniques used by archaeologists. Admission is free apart from the Timequest gallery for which there is a small charge.

Museum of Antiquities – University of Newcastle upon Tyne

This museum features finds from many of the sites on Hadrian's Wall, including Wallsend. it has a particularly fine collection of Latin inscriptions.

There are Roman remains visible at Benwell to the west of Newcastle, including a temple to Antenociticus.

Of related interest is the museum of Bede's World at Jarrow which features reconstructions of early medieval timber buildings. Closer to home in North Tyneside is the Stephenson Railway Museum, which includes stock that once ran on the former riverside railway line immediately to the south of the fort site.

Further reading

Books relevant to the site can be found in the museum shop. The following volumes are recommended as being of particular interest:

Hadrian's Wall

The best introduction to the history of the northern frontier is *Hadrian's Wall* by D.J. Breeze and B. Dobson (Penguin, revised edition 2000). Among the many excellent guides is *Hadrian's Wall: A souvenir guide to the Roman Wall* by English Heritage (revised edition 2000). For an outline of recent research and discoveries the 1999 Hadrian's Wall Pilgrimage book, *Hadrian's Wall 1989-1999* edited by Paul Bidwell, is invaluable.

Roman Britain

The clearest and most readable account of Roman Britain in general is *Britannia* by S.S. Frere (Pimlico, revised edition 1987). Joan Alcock's *Life in Roman Britain* (English Heritage/Batsford 1996) provides a clear commentary on social conditions in the province.

The Roman Army

Peter Connolly has produced several excellent illustrated books on the Roman Army, including *The Legionary* (Oxford University Press, 1988), *The Cavalryman* (Oxford University Press 1988) and *The Roman Fort* (Oxford University Press, 1991). The most up to date statement of knowledge about forts is *Roman Forts in Britain* by P.T. Bidwell (English Heritage/Batsford, 1997), which includes direct reference to Segedunum.

Segedunum

The accounts of the excavations of 1975-84 and the more recent excavations of 1997-9 are currently being prepared for publication and should shortly be available. Summaries of the excavations can be found in the handbooks of the Hadrian's Wall Pilgrimage. For the 1975-84 excavations: *The Eleventh Pilgrimage of Hadrian's Wall*, edited by Charles Daniels (1989), pages 77-83. For the more recent work: *Hadrian's Wall 1989-1999*, edited by Paul Bidwell (1999), pages 83-97.

Wallsend

A History of the Parish of Wallsend, by W. Richardson (1923, reprinted by Newcastle City and North Tyneside Libraries in 1998) provides an excellent account of the history of the borough, particularly in the eighteenth and nineteenth centuries. In addition North Tyneside and Newcastle Libraries have published a number of booklets on various aspects of the recent history of Wallsend including *Wallsend Colliery Pit Disaster 18th June 1835* by Ken and Pauline Hutchinson. For a detailed account of the excavations on the site of Wallsend B pit see *Excavations at Wallsend Colliery B pit, 1997* in *Archaeologia Aeliana*, fifth series, vol 26, 1998, by R. Oram, W.B. Griffiths and N. Hodgson.

Glossary

Aedes
A shrine, found at the centre of the rear range of the headquarters building. The standards of the garrison would be kept there when not in use.

Auxiliary
Non citizen soldier. Such troops made up the garrison of Hadrian's Wall, and would be rewarded with citizenship of the Roman Empire on their retirement.

Balineum
Also spelt *Balneum*, the bath-house.

Caldarium
The hot room of the bath-house.

Centurion
Commander of a body of infantry, the century, of 80 men.

Cippi
Defensive entanglement made from sharpened branches.

Cohort
Auxiliary unit of either infantry or infantry and cavalry, usually 500 or 1000 men.

Cohors equitata
Mixed unit of six centuries of infantry and four *turmae* of cavalry.

Contubernium
Subdivision of a century or *turma*, group of men sharing a two roomed section of a barrack.

Decurion
Commander of a cavalry *turma* of around 30 men.

Frigidarium
Cold room in the bath-house.

Horrea
Granaries, in which the food supplies for the fort would be kept.

Hypocaust
The heating system in which hot air circulates below the floor before passing through hollow tiles in the walls to jacket a room in heat.

Labrum
Basin with small fountain at its centre in the hot room of the bath-house. Water would flow constantly to run across the floor and turn to steam.

Legionary
Citizen soldier. Legions consisted of around 5,000 men. The legionaries were skilled troops, and were responsible for the construction of Hadrian's Wall and the fort at Segedunum.

Medicus
A medical officer.

Porta
Gateway.

Praefectus
The commanding officer of an auxiliary cohort. Such a post would often be the starting point for a high career within the Empire.

Praefurnium
The boiler house of the baths. This would have been an unpleasant place to work due to the smoke and soot that built up within it.

Praetorium
The Commanding Officer's private residence within the fort. He would be accompanied by his wife and family as well as staff and servants.

Principia
The headquarters building of the fort. The unit's funds were kept here as were its standards. The garrison's adminstration was handled from this building.

Tepidarium
The warm room of the bath-house.

Turma
A cavalry troop of around 30 men.

Valetudinarium
Hospital.

Vicus
The civilian settlement outside a fort.